LOW GLYCEMIC
COOKBOOK

MEGA BUNDLE – 3 Manuscripts in 1 – 120+ Low Glycemic - friendly recipes including Salad, Casseroles and pizza

TABLE OF CONTENTS

SIDE DISHES 9

SPICY SHRIMP STIR FRY 9

ARTICHOKE AND SPINACH PIZZA 10

MINT PIZZA..11

SAUSAGE PIZZA 12

BEEF & BROCCOLI STIR FRY 13

GINGER CHICKEN SOUP..14

CILANTRO SKEWERS 15

CURRY SHRIMP...16

ORANGE ROUGHY 17

LEMON TILAPIA 18

MEDITERRANEAN SEA BASS..19

WASABI WHITEFISH 20

CAJUN CHICKEN 21

BASIL CHICKEN SANDWICH 22

MARINARA CHICKEN 23

EDAMAME FRITATTA 24

LEEKS FRITATTA..25

MUSHROOM FRITATTA 26

PEAS FRITATTA 27

BELL PEPPER FRITATTA..28

POTATO FRITATTA...29

SKILLET PIZZA 30

GLAZED PORK CHOPS..31

PANINI CHICKEN...32

PENNE PASTA 33

TURKEY SANDWICH 34

ROASTED SQUASH 35

BRUSSELS SPROUT CHIPS 36

BEET CHIPS 37

SPINACH CHIPS 38

KALE CHIPS 39

EGGPLANT CHIPS 40

TOMATO CHIPS 41

PASTA 42

SIMPLE SPAGHETTI 42

SALAD 44

COUSCOUS SALAD 44

POTATO SALAD 46

CARROT SALAD 47

MOROCCAN SALAD 48

AVOCADO CHICKEN SALAD 50

CUCUMBER SALAD 52

MANGO SALAD 54

RICE SALAD 56

SECOND COOKBOOK 58

SOUP RECIPES 59

ZUCCHINI SOUP 59

BROCCOLI SOUP 60

CHICKEN NOODLE SOUP 62

TORTILLA SOUP 64

ASPARAGUS SOUP 65

LENTIL SOUP 66

BROCCOLI AND RED CAPSICUM SOUP 68

CANTALOUPE SOUP 69

SIDE DISHES 70

GREEN PESTO PASTA...70

BUCKWHEAT DOSA 71

ZUCCHINI BAJRA KHICHDI 72

QUINOA MUTHIA 74

LIME GRILLED CORN...76

CAPSICUM AND PANEER SUBZI 77

AVOCADO DIP 79

ONION PURIS..80

KALE CHIPS 81

CRANBERRY SALAD 82

ITALIAN SALAD 83

CHICKPEA COLESLAW..84

ROMAINE SALAD 85

GRAIN SALAD 86

QUINOA SALAD 87

WEDGE SALAD...88

COUSCOUS SALAD..89

FARRO SALAD 90

THAI MANGO SALAD 91

LENTIL FRITATTA 92

SPINACH FRITATTA 93

BLACK BEAN FRITATTA 94

CHEESE FRITATTA...95

BROCCOLI FRITATTA...96

SHAKSHUKA...97

BROCCOLI CASSEROLE..98

BEAN FRITATTA 99

ROASTED SQUASH...100

POTATO CHIPS...101

ZUCCHINI CHIPS 102

PIZZA RECIPES 103

ZUCCHINI PIZZA CRUST 103

BARBEQUE PIZZA..105

SHRIMP PIZZA...106

CAULIFLOWER CRUST PIZZA...107

THIRD COOKBOOK..109

ROAST RECIPES 110

ROASTED ONION 110

ROASTED SQUASH...111

ROASTED GARLIC...112

SOUP RECIPES 113

ZUCCHINI SOUP..113

CREAMY CAULIFLOWER SOUP 114

SWEET POTATO SOUP 115

SIDE DISHES 116

GREEN PESTO PASTA...116

FAJITA LETTUCE WRAPS...117

FAJITAS WITH BASIL SAUCE...119

BRUSEELS SPROUTS WITH BALSAMIC GLAZE 121

ROASTED SWEET POTATOES 123

SPAGHETTI SQUASH PLATTER 124

ROASTED CAULIFLOWER AND RICE PLATTER..............................126

SALAD WITH KALE CAULIFLOWER..127

GRAIN FREE FAJITAS 129

LIME SPINACH CHIPS 131

AIP BREADSTICKS 132

CAULIFLOWER RICE 134

GLAZED SALMON 135

BISON STEW 136

GARLIC AND HERB SCALLOPS 137

ROASTED ROSEMARY BEETS 138

BACON-WRAPPED SHRIMP 139

PORK CHOPS WITH ONION 140

BACON & KALE 141

GREEK SALAD 142

QUINOA AND LENTIL SALAD 143

CRANBERRY & SPINACH SALAD 144

KALE SALAD 145

TORTELLINI SALAD 146

TACO SALAD 147

DORITO TACO SALAD 148

CHEESEBURGER SALAD 149

MANDARIN SALAD 150

SOUTHWESTERN SALAD...151

STEW RECIPES 152

BUTTERNUT SQUASH STEW 152

BEEF STEW 154

CASSEROLE RECIPES 156

CORN CASSEROLE..156

ARTICHOKE CASSEROLE..158

PIZZA RECIPES 159

MUSHROOM PIZZA 159

CASEROLE PIZZA 161

clarifying purposes only and are the owned by the owners themselves, not affiliated with this document.

Introduction

Low Glycemic recipes for personal enjoyment but also for family enjoyment. You will love them for sure for how easy it is to prepare them.

SPICY SHRIMP STIR FRY

Serves: **1**

Prep Time: **10** Minutes

Cook Time: **10** Minutes

Total Time: **20** Minutes

INGREDIENTS

- 1 orange
- Cayenne powder
- 3 oz shrimp
- Ginger powder
- 4 tbs vegetable stock
- Curry powder
- 25 cups red onion
- 1 cup cabbage
- Garlic powder

DIRECTIONS

1. Coat the shrimp in the seasonings.
2. Pour the broth into a pan, then add cabbage, onion, and shrimp.
3. Cook until the shrimp turns pink.
4. Serve topped with orange juice and orange slices.

ARTICHOKE AND SPINACH PIZZA

Serves: *6-8*

Prep Time: *10*   Minutes

Cook Time: *15*   Minutes

Total Time: *25*   Minutes

INGREDIENTS

- 1 pizza crust
- 1 garlic clove
- ½ lb. spinach
- ½ lb. soft cheese
- 2 oz. artichoke hearts
- 1 cup mozzarella cheese
- 1 tablespoon olive oil

DIRECTIONS

1. Spread tomato sauce on the pizza crust
2. Place all the toppings on the pizza crust
3. Bake the pizza at 425 F for 12-15 minutes
4. When ready remove pizza from the oven and serve

MINT PIZZA

Serves: **6-8**

Prep Time: **10**   Minutes

Cook Time: **15**   Minutes

Total Time: **25**   Minutes

INGREDIENTS

- 1 pizza crust
- 1 olive oil
- 1 garlic clove
- 1 cup mozzarella cheese
- 2 oz. mint
- 2 courgettes

DIRECTIONS

1. Spread tomato sauce on the pizza crust
2. Place all the toppings on the pizza crust
3. Bake the pizza at 425 F for 12-15 minutes
4. When ready remove pizza from the oven and serve

SAUSAGE PIZZA

Serves: **6-8**

Prep Time: **10** Minutes

Cook Time: **15** Minutes

Total Time: **25** Minutes

INGREDIENTS

- 2 pork sausages
- 1 tablespoon olive oil
- 2 garlic cloves
- 1 tsp fennel seeds
- ½ lb. ricotta
- 1 cup mozzarella cheese
- 1 oz. parmesan cheese
- 1 pizza crust

DIRECTIONS

1. Spread tomato sauce on the pizza crust
2. Place all the toppings on the pizza crust
3. Bake the pizza at 425 F for 12-15 minutes
4. When ready remove pizza from the oven and serve

BEEF & BROCCOLI STIR FRY

Serves: **4**

Prep Time: **10**   Minutes

Cook Time: **30**   Minutes

Total Time: **40**   Minutes

INGREDIENTS

- 2 cloves garlic
- ½ lb Beef Sirloin steaks
- Chicken broth
- 2 tbs liquid Aminos
- 1 tsp onion powder
- 1 tbs parsley
- 2 cups broccoli florets

DIRECTIONS

1. Sauté the beef in a few tbs of chicken broth until brown.
2. Add onion powder, garlic, broccoli, liquid aminos and parsley.
3. Saute until well done.
4. Serve immediately.

Serves: *1*
Prep Time: 5   Minutes

Cook Time: 15   Minutes

Total Time: 20   Minutes

INGREDIENTS

- 2 cloves garlic
- Salt
- Pepper
- 3 stalks celery
- 3 oz chicken tenders
- 4 cups chicken broth
- 4 slices ginger

DIRECTIONS

1. Bring the broth to a boil.
2. Add the garlic, ginger, and celery.
3. Simmer for 5 minutes.
4. Add in the chicken and boil for 10 more minutes.
5. Season with salt and pepper.
6. Serve immediately.

CILANTRO SKEWERS

Serves: **1**

Prep Time: **20** Minutes

Cook Time: **120** Minutes

Total Time: **140** Minutes

INGREDIENTS

- Cherry tomatoes
- Red pepper flakes
- Salt
- Pepper
- 2 tbs lemon juice
- Cilantro
- 100g shrimp

DIRECTIONS

1. Mix the cilantro, red pepper flakes, salt, pepper and shrimp together.
2. Marinade for at least 2 hours.
3. Place on skewers alternating with tomatoes.
4. Cook on a barbeque.
5. Season with salt and pepper.
6. Serve immediately.

Serves: **14**

Prep Time: **10**   Minutes

Cook Time: **10**   Minutes

Total Time: **20**   Minutes

INGREDIENTS

- 1/8 cup water
- 100g shrimp
- 1 onion
- Pepper
- 1/ tsp curry powder
- ¼ tsp cumin
- Salt
- 4 garlic cloves

DIRECTIONS

1. Cook the garlic and onion until translucent.
2. Add in the shrimp, seasonings and water.
3. Cook until done.
4. Serve immediately.

ORANGE ROUGHY

Serves: *1*

Prep Time: *10*   Minutes

Cook Time: *15*   Minutes

Total Time: *25*   Minutes

INGREDIENTS

- 100g orange roughy fillet
- 2 tbs lemon juice
- 1 tsp thyme
- 1 tsp rosemary
- ¼ tsp onion powder
- Salt
- Pepper

DIRECTIONS

1. Place the ingredients in a baking dish and cover with tin foil.
2. Bake at 350F for 15 minutes.
3. Serve hot.

Serves: *1*

Prep Time: *10*   Minutes

Cook Time: *20*   Minutes

Total Time: *30*   Minutes

INGREDIENTS

- ¼ cup lemon juice
- 1 lemon zest
- 100g tilapia
- 1 tbs onion
- 1 tsp dill
- Salt
- Pepper

DIRECTIONS

1. Place the ingredients in a tin foil, then wrap them up.
2. Cook on a grill until done
3. Serve when ready

MEDITERRANEAN SEA BASS

Serves: *1*

Prep Time: *10*   Minutes

Cook Time: *10*   Minutes

Total Time: *20*   Minutes

INGREDIENTS

- 100g sea Bass
- 2 cloves garlic
- 1 lemon juice
- 1 lemon zest
- 1 tbs onion
- ½ tsp parsley
- Salt
- Pepper

DIRECTIONS

1. Place the ingredients in a tin foil bag.
2. Cook on the barbeque for 10 minutes.
3. Serve topped with fresh parsley.

Serves: *1*

Prep Time: *10*   Minutes

Cook Time: *5*   Minutes

Total Time: *15*   Minutes

INGREDIENTS

- ½ tsp ginger
- 100g whitefish
- 1 tbs mustard
- 1 tsp wasabi powder

DIRECTIONS

1. Mix the mustard with the wasabi powder.
2. Add the ginger.
3. Coat the fish with the mixture.
4. Allow to sit for at least half an hour.
5. Grill for 5 minutes.
6. Serve hot.

CAJUN CHICKEN

Serves: *1*

Prep Time: *5*   Minutes

Cook Time: *25*   Minutes

Total Time: *30*   Minutes

INGREDIENTS

- ½ tbs milk
- ½ tsp Cajun seasoning
- 100g chicken

DIRECTIONS

1. Preheat the oven to 350F.
2. Coat the chicken with milk.
3. Sprinkle with Cajun seasoning.
4. Bake for 25 minutes.
5. Serve immediately.

Serves: *1*
Prep Time: 5   Minutes
Cook Time: *0*   Minutes
Total Time: 5   Minutes

INGREDIENTS

- ½ tomato
- 1 toast
- 100g chicken
- Basil
- Salt
- Pepper

DIRECTIONS

1. Cook the chicken, allow to chill, then shred.
2. Arrange the ingredients on top of the toast.
3. Serve immediately.

Serves: *1*

Prep Time: **10**   Minutes

Cook Time: **25**   Minutes

Total Time: **35**   Minutes

INGREDIENTS

- ½ tsp oregano
- Parsley
- 100g chicken
- 1 toast
- ½ tsp basil
- 3 garlic cloves
- 2 tsp onion
- Salt
- Pepper

DIRECTIONS

1. Crush the toast and combine with oregano, basil, salt, and pepper.
2. Coat the chicken with the mixture and place in a casserole dish.
3. Cook covered for 25 minutes at 375F.
4. Serve topped with marinara sauce and parsley.

EDAMAME FRITATTA

Serves: **2**

Prep Time: **10**   Minutes

Cook Time: **20**   Minutes

Total Time: **30**   Minutes

INGREDIENTS

- 1 cup edamame
- 1 tablespoon olive oil
- ½ red onion
- 2 eggs
- ¼ tsp salt
- 2 oz. cheddar cheese
- 1 garlic clove
- ¼ tsp dill

DIRECTIONS

1. In a bowl whisk eggs with salt and cheese
2. In a frying pan heat olive oil and pour egg mixture
3. Add remaining ingredients and mix well
4. Serve when ready

LEEKS FRITATTA

Serves: **2**

Prep Time: **10** Minutes

Cook Time: **20** Minutes

Total Time: **30** Minutes

INGREDIENTS

- ½ lb. leek
- 1 tablespoon olive oil
- ½ red onion
- ¼ tsp salt
- 2 eggs
- 2 oz. cheddar cheese
- 1 garlic clove
- ¼ tsp dill

DIRECTIONS

1. In a bowl whisk eggs with salt and cheese
2. In a frying pan heat olive oil and pour egg mixture
3. Add remaining ingredients and mix well
4. Serve when ready

MUSHROOM FRITATTA

Serves: **2**

Prep Time: **10**   Minutes

Cook Time: **20**   Minutes

Total Time: **30**   Minutes

INGREDIENTS

- ½ lb. mushrooms
- 1 tablespoon olive oil
- ½ red onion
- ¼ tsp salt
- 2 eggs
- 2 oz. cheddar cheese
- 1 garlic clove
- ¼ tsp dill

DIRECTIONS

1. In a bowl whisk eggs with salt and cheese
2. In a frying pan heat olive oil and pour egg mixture
3. Add remaining ingredients and mix well
4. Serve when ready

PEAS FRITATTA

Serves: **2**

Prep Time: **10** Minutes

Cook Time: **20** Minutes

Total Time: **30** Minutes

INGREDIENTS

- 1 cup peas
- 1 tablespoon olive oil
- ½ red onion
- ¼ tsp salt
- 2 eggs
- 2 oz. cheddar cheese
- 1 garlic clove
- ¼ tsp dill

DIRECTIONS

1. In a bowl whisk eggs with salt and cheese
2. In a frying pan heat olive oil and pour egg mixture
3. Add remaining ingredients and mix well
4. Serve when ready.

Serves: **2**

Prep Time: **10** Minutes

Cook Time: **20** Minutes

Total Time: **30** Minutes

INGREDIENTS

- 1 cup red bell pepper
- 1 tablespoon olive oil
- ½ red onion
- ¼ tsp salt
- 2 eggs
- 2 oz. parmesan cheese
- 1 garlic clove
- ¼ tsp dill

DIRECTIONS

1. In a bowl whisk eggs with salt and cheese
2. In a frying pan heat olive oil and pour egg mixture
3. Add remaining ingredients and mix well
4. Serve when ready.

POTATO FRITATTA

Serves: **2**

Prep Time: **10** Minutes

Cook Time: **20** Minutes

Total Time: **30** Minutes

INGREDIENTS

- 1 cup sweet potato
- 1 tablespoon olive oil
- ½ red onion
- ¼ tsp salt
- 2 eggs
- 2 oz. cheddar cheese
- 1 garlic clove
- ¼ tsp dill

DIRECTIONS

1. In a bowl whisk eggs with salt and cheese
2. In a frying pan heat olive oil and pour egg mixture
3. Add remaining ingredients and mix well
4. Serve when ready

SKILLET PIZZA

Serves: *1*

Prep Time: *10*   Minutes

Cook Time: *20*   Minutes

Total Time: *30*   Minutes

INGREDIENTS

- ¼ red onion
- ½ cup red bell pepper
- ¼ tsp salt
- 2 eggs
- 1 cup tomato sauce
- 1 cup mozzarella cheese
- 1 pizza crust

DIRECTIONS

1. On a pizza crust spread tomato sauce
2. Add toppings on pizza
3. Place pizza in the skillet and cover with a lid
4. Cook on low heat for 18-20 minutes or until pizza is ready

GLAZED PORK CHOPS

Serves: **4**

Prep Time: **10** Minutes

Cook Time: **15** Minutes

Total Time: **25** Minutes

INGREDIENTS

- 1 cup all-purpose flour
- 4 pork loin chops
- ½ cup maple syrup
- 1 tablespoon cornstarch
- 1 cup brown sugar
- pinch of salt
- 2 tablespoons water

DIRECTIONS

1. In a bowl combine salt and flour together
2. Place the pork chops in the bowl and turn to coat
3. Place pork chops in a skillet and cook until golden brown
4. Add maple syrup, sugar, water cornstarch, and bring to a boil
5. Cook until the sugar is dissolved and meat is cooked
6. When ready remove from the skillet and serve

PANINI CHICKEN

Serves: **1**

Prep Time: **10** Minutes

Cook Time: **15** Minutes

Total Time: **25** Minutes

INGREDIENTS

- 1 lb. chicken breast
- 1 tsp gingerroot
- ½ cup chicken broth
- ¼ tsp salt
- ¼ tsp turmeric
- 4 green onion

DIRECTIONS

1. In a slow cooker place your chicken and add broth, garlic clove, green onions and gingerroot
2. When ready remove chicken mixture and place the chicken on a flatbread
3. Cook sandwich in a panini maker
4. When ready remove and serve

PENNE PASTA

Serves: **2**
Prep Time: **10**   Minutes

Cook Time: **20**   Minutes

Total Time: **30**   Minutes

INGREDIENTS

- 1 package penne pasta
- 1 onion
- 1 tablespoon thyme
- 1 tablespoon basil
- ¼ cup white wine
- 1 tablespoon tomato paste
- 1 tablespoon all-purpose flour
- 1 cup parmesan cheese

DIRECTIONS

1. In a stockpot cook pasta al dente
2. In a skillet sauté onion until soft, add salt, herbs, tomato paste, flour and cook for 2-3 minutes
3. Add pasta to the tomato mixture and bring to a boil
4. When ready serve with parmesan cheese on top

TURKEY SANDWICH

Serves: *1*

Prep Time: *5* Minutes

Cook Time: *5* Minutes

Total Time: *10* Minutes

INGREDIENTS

- 2 oz. cream cheese
- 2 tablespoons salad dressing
- 1 tsp garlic powder
- 1 loaf bread
- Lettuce
- 1 lb. cooked turkey
- ½ lb. swiss cheese
- 1 tomato

DIRECTIONS

1. In a bowl combine cream cheese, garlic powder and salad dressing
2. Spread mixture on the bread
3. Add lettuce, tomatoes, cheese and turkey
4. Serve when ready

ROASTED SQUASH

Serves: **3-4**

Prep Time: **10** Minutes

Cook Time: **20** Minutes

Total Time: **30** Minutes

INGREDIENTS

- 2 delicata squashes
- 2 tablespoons olive oil
- 1 tsp curry powder
- 1 tsp salt

DIRECTIONS

1. Preheat the oven to 400 F
2. Cut everything in half lengthwise
3. Toss everything with olive oil and place onto a prepared baking sheet
4. Roast for 18-20 minutes at 400 F or until golden brown
5. When ready remove from the oven and serve

Serves: 2

Prep Time: *10*   Minutes

Cook Time: *20*   Minutes

Total Time: *30*   Minutes

INGREDIENTS

- 1 lb. brussels sprouts
- 1 tablespoon olive oil
- 1 tablespoon parmesan cheese
- 1 tsp garlic powder
- 1 tsp seasoning

DIRECTIONS

1. Preheat the oven to 425 F
2. In a bowl toss everything with olive oil and seasoning
3. Spread everything onto a prepared baking sheet
4. Bake for 8-10 minutes or until crisp
5. When ready remove from the oven and serve

Serves: **2**

Prep Time: **10**   Minutes

Cook Time: **20**   Minutes

Total Time: **30**   Minutes

INGREDIENTS

- 1 lb. beet
- 1 tablespoon olive oil
- 1 tablespoon parmesan cheese
- 1 tsp garlic powder
- 1 tsp seasoning

DIRECTIONS

1. Preheat the oven to 425 F
2. In a bowl toss everything with olive oil and seasoning
3. Spread everything onto a prepared baking sheet
4. Bake for 8-10 minutes or until crisp
5. When ready remove from the oven and serve

SPINACH CHIPS

Serves: **2**

Prep Time: **10** Minutes

Cook Time: **20** Minutes

Total Time: **30** Minutes

INGREDIENTS

- 1 lb. spinach
- 1 tablespoon olive oil
- 1 tablespoon parmesan cheese
- 1 tsp garlic powder
- 1 tsp seasoning

DIRECTIONS

1. Preheat the oven to 425 F
2. In a bowl toss everything with olive oil and seasoning
3. Spread everything onto a prepared baking sheet
4. Bake for 8-10 minutes or until crisp
5. When ready remove from the oven and serve

KALE CHIPS

Serves: **2**
Prep Time: **10**   Minutes

Cook Time: **20**   Minutes

Total Time: **30**   Minutes

INGREDIENTS

- 1 lb. kale
- 1 tablespoon olive oil
- 1 tablespoon parmesan cheese
- 1 tsp garlic powder
- 1 tsp seasoning

DIRECTIONS

1. Preheat the oven to 425 F
2. In a bowl toss everything with olive oil and seasoning
3. Spread everything onto a prepared baking sheet
4. Bake for 8-10 minutes or until crisp
5. When ready remove from the oven and serve

Serves: *2*

Prep Time: *10*   Minutes

Cook Time: *20*   Minutes

Total Time: *30*   Minutes

INGREDIENTS

- 1 lb. eggplant
- 1 tablespoon olive oil
- 1 tablespoon parmesan cheese
- 1 tsp garlic powder
- 1 tsp seasoning

DIRECTIONS

1. Preheat the oven to 425 F
2. In a bowl toss everything with olive oil and seasoning
3. Spread everything onto a prepared baking sheet
4. Bake for 8-10 minutes or until crisp
5. When ready remove from the oven and serve

TOMATO CHIPS

Serves: *2*
Prep Time: *10*   Minutes

Cook Time: *20*   Minutes

Total Time: *30*   Minutes

INGREDIENTS

- 1 lb. tomato
- 1 tablespoon olive oil
- 1 tablespoon parmesan cheese
- 1 tsp garlic powder
- 1 tsp seasoning

DIRECTIONS

1. Preheat the oven to 425 F
2. In a bowl toss everything with olive oil and seasoning
3. Spread everything onto a prepared baking sheet
4. Bake for 8-10 minutes or until crisp
5. When ready remove from the oven and serve

PASTA

SIMPLE SPAGHETTI

Serves: 2

Prep Time: 5   Minutes

Cook Time: 15   Minutes

Total Time: 20   Minutes

INGREDIENTS

- 10 oz. spaghetti
- 2 eggs
- ½ cup parmesan cheese
- 1 tsp black pepper
- Olive oil
- 1 tsp parsley
- 2 cloves garlic

DIRECTIONS

1. In a pot boil spaghetti (or any other type of pasta), drain and set aside
2. In a bowl whish eggs with parmesan cheese
3. In a skillet heat olive oil, add garlic and cook for 1-2 minutes
4. Pour egg mixture and mix well
5. Add pasta and stir well

6. When ready garnish with parsley and serve

SALAD

COUSCOUS SALAD

Serves: *5*

Prep Time: *10*   Minutes

Cook Time: *50*   Minutes

Total Time: *60*   Minutes

INGREDIENTS
Salad
- Spinach leaves
- Seasonings
- ½ pumpkin
- 1 cup cous cous
- 2 chicken breasts

Dressing
- 2 tbs vinegar
- 3 tbs olive oil
- 2 tbs mustard
- 4 tbs mayonnaise
- 2 tbs lemon juice
- Pepper
- Salt

DIRECTIONS

1. Peel and cut the pumpkin
2. Toss in oil and season
3. Roast in oven for at least 30 minutes
4. Grill the chicken
5. Cook the cous cous
6. Mix the dressing ingredients together
7. Mix everyting together in a salad bowl
8. Serve

POTATO SALAD

Serves: 2

Prep Time: 5   Minutes

Cook Time: 10   Minutes

Total Time: 15   Minutes

INGREDIENTS

- 5 potatoes
- 1 tsp cumin seeds
- 1/3 cup oil
- 2 tsp mustard
- 1 red onion
- 2 cloves garlic
- 1/3 cup lemon juice
- 1 tsp sea salt

DIRECTIONS

1. Steam the potatoes until tender
2. Mix mustard, turmeric powder, lemon juice, cumin seeds, and salt
3. Place the potatoes in a bowl and pour the lemon mixture over
4. Add the chopped onion and minced garlic over
5. Stir to coat and refrigerate covered
6. Add oil and stir before serving

CARROT SALAD

Serves: 2

Prep Time: 5   Minutes

Cook Time: 5   Minutes

Total Time: *10*   Minutes

INGREDIENTS

- 1 ½ tbs lemon juice
- 1/3 tsp salt
- ¼ tsp black pepper
- 2 tbs olive oil
- 1/3 lb carrots
- 1 tsp mustard

DIRECTIONS

1. Mix mustard, lemon juice and oil together
2. Peel and shred the carrots in a bowl
3. Stir in the dressing and season with salt and pepper
4. Mix well and allow to chill for at least 30 minutes
5. Serve

MOROCCAN SALAD

Serves: 2

Prep Time: 5   Minutes

Cook Time: 5   Minutes

Total Time: **10**   Minutes

INGREDIENTS

- 2 tbs lemon juice
- 1 tsp cumin
- 1 tsp paprika
- 3 tbs olive oil
- 2 cloves garlic
- 5 carrots
- Salt
- Pepper

DIRECTIONS

1. Peel and slice the carrots
2. Add the carrots in boiled water and simmer for at least 5 minutes
3. Drain and rinse the carrots under cold water
4. Add in a bowl
5. Mix the lemon juice, garlic, cumin, paprika, and olive oil together

6. Pour the mixture over the carrots and toss then season with salt and pepper

7. Serve immediately

AVOCADO CHICKEN SALAD

Serves: 2
Prep Time: 5   Minutes

Cook Time: 5   Minutes

Total Time: **10** Minutes

INGREDIENTS

- 3 tsp lime juice
- 3 tbs cilantro
- 1 chicken breast
- 1 avocado
- 1/3 cup onion
- 1 apple
- 1 cup celery
- Salt
- Pepper
- Olive oil

DIRECTIONS

1. Dice the chicken breast
2. Season with salt and pepper and cook into a greased skillet until golden
3. Dice the vegetables and place over the chicken in a bowl
4. Mash the avocado and sprinkle in the cilantro

5. Season with salt and pepper and add lime juice
6. Serve drizzled with olive oil

CUCUMBER SALAD

Serves:	*8*
Prep Time:	*5* Minutes
Cook Time:	*5* Minutes
Total Time:	*10* Minutes

INGREDIENTS

- 2 cucumbers
- ½ cup vinegar
- 2 tsp sugar
- 1/3 cup water
- 2 tbs sour cream
- ½ tbs salt
- 1 ½ tsp paprika
- ½ onion

DIRECTIONS

1. Peel and slice the cucumbers
2. Place the cucumbers on a baking sheet and sprinkle with salt
3. Allow to chill for about 30 minutes then squeeze out the excess water
4. Place the onion slices in a bowl and add the drained cucumbers over
5. Add water, sugar, vinegar and paprika

6. Allow to marinate for at least 2 hours
7. Serve

MANGO SALAD

Serves: **4**

Prep Time: **10** Minutes

Cook Time: **5** Minutes

Total Time: **15** Minutes

INGREDIENTS
Salad
- Salad leaves
- 2 chicken breasts
- 2 mangoes
- 2 avocados
- 2 tbs pine nuts

Dressing
- 3 tbs oil
- Salt
- Pepper
- 2 tbs lemon juice
- 3 tbs orange juice
- 1 tsp mustard

DIRECTIONS

1. Divide the salat onto 4 plates
2. Slice the peeled mango and place over the salad
3. Peel and slice the avocado then place it on top

4. Grill the chicken, dice it and place it over

5. Mix the dressing ingredients together and pour over

6. Serve immediately

RICE SALAD

Serves: *4*

Prep Time: *10*   Minutes

Cook Time: *5*   Minutes

Total Time: *15*   Minutes

INGREDIENTS
Salad
- 3 tbs basil leaves
- 100g Kalamata olives
- 3 tbs pine nuts
- 2 green shallots
- ½ sun dried tomato
- 1 cup rice

Dressing
- 3 tbs oil
- Pepper
- 2 tbs mustard
- 3 tbs lemon juice
- Salt
- 1 clove garlic

DIRECTIONS

1. Cook the rice
2. Mix the dressing ingredients together

3. Mix the salad ingredients with the rice in a bowl
4. Add the dressing and serve

SECOND COOKBOOK

ZUCCHINI SOUP

Serves: **4**
Prep Time: **10**   Minutes

Cook Time: **20**   Minutes

Total Time: **30**   Minutes

INGREDIENTS

- 1 tablespoon olive oil
- 1 lb. zucchini
- ¼ red onion
- ½ cup all-purpose flour
- ¼ tsp salt
- ¼ tsp pepper
- 1 can vegetable broth
- 1 cup heavy cream

DIRECTIONS

1. In a saucepan heat olive oil and sauté zucchini until tender
2. Add remaining ingredients to the saucepan and bring to a boil
3. When all the vegetables are tender transfer to a blender and blend until smooth
4. Pour soup into bowls, garnish with parsley and serve

BROCCOLI SOUP

Serves: 2

Prep Time: *10*   Minutes

Cook Time: *10*   Minutes

Total Time: *20*   Minutes

INGREDIENTS

- 1 onion
- 2 cloves garlic
- 1 tbs butter
- 2 cup broccoli
- 1 potato
- 3 cup chicken broth
- 1 cup cheddar cheese
- 1/3 cup buttermilk
- Salt
- Pepper

DIRECTIONS

1. Cook the onion and garlic in melted butter for 5 minutes
2. Add the diced potato, broccoli florets and chicken broth
3. Bring to a boil, then reduce the heat and simmer for at least 5 minutes
4. Allow to cool, then pulse until smooth using a blender

5. Return to the saucepan and add the buttermilk and ¼ cup cheese
6. Cook for about 3 minutes
7. Season with salt and pepper
8. Serve topped with the remaining cheese

CHICKEN NOODLE SOUP

Serves: *6*

Prep Time: *40*   Minutes

Cook Time: *80*   Minutes

Total Time: *120*   Minutes

INGREDIENTS

Broth:
- 15 peppercorns
- 2 onions
- 2 carrots
- 1 rib celery
- 3 sprigs thyme
- 5 cloves garlic
- 3 bay leaves
- 8 chicken thighs

Soup:
- 2 chicken bouillon cubes
- 1 tsp salt
- 5 oz egg noodles
- 1/3 cup parsley
- 2 ribs celery
- 2 carrots

DIRECTIONS

1. Place the broth ingredients in a pot with 12 cups of water
2. Bring to a boil, then reduce the heat and simmer for about 20 minutes
3. Remove the chicken and shred meat from bones
4. Return the bones to the pot and continue to simmer for another 60 minutes
5. Strain the broth and discard the bones and other solids
6. Skim broth and bring to a boil
7. Add the soup ingredients except for the parsley
8. Stir in the noodles and cook for at least 5 minutes
9. Stir in the chicken meat and parsley and cook 1 more minute
10. Serve immediately

Serves: **6**

Prep Time: **10** Minutes

Cook Time: **10** Minutes

Total Time: **20** Minutes

INGREDIENTS

- 1/3 cup rice
- 15 oz salsa
- 1 can black beans
- 30 oz chicken broth
- 1 cup corn
- Chicken

DIRECTIONS

1. Place the broth and the salsa in a pot and bring to a boil
2. Add rice, beans and cooked chicken
3. Simmer covered for about 10 minutes
4. Stir in the corn
5. Serve topped with cheese

ASPARAGUS SOUP

Serves: **4**
Prep Time: **15**   Minutes

Cook Time: **35**   Minutes

Total Time: **50**   Minutes

INGREDIENTS

- 2 tbs oil
- 1/3 tsp salt
- 1 cup bread cubes
- 1 cup potato
- 2 tsp horseradish
- 3 cups chicken broth
- 1 lb asparagus
- Scallions
- 1 shallot

DIRECTIONS

1. Cook the shallot until soft for 2 minutes
2. Add the asparagus, potato, broth, horseradish and salt and bring to a boil
3. Reduce the heat and simmer for about 15 minutes
4. Pulse using a blender
5. Cook the bread cubes in hot oil until crispy, serve with croutons

LENTIL SOUP

Serves: *9*

Prep Time: *10* Minutes

Cook Time: *50* Minutes

Total Time: *60* Minutes

INGREDIENTS

- 2 tbs oil
- 1 stalk celery
- 1 red bell pepper
- 2 cans chicken broth
- 1 onion
- 1 cup carrots
- 2 garlic cloves
- 2 tsp cumin
- 1 tsp coriander
- 1 can tomatoes
- 2 sweet potatoes
- 3 tsp thyme leaves
- 2 cups red lentils

DIRECTIONS

1. Cook the onion, celery, carrots and red pepper in hot oil for 3 minutes

2. Add garlic, thyme, cumin and coriander and cook for 10 more minutes

3. Add the broth, sweet potatoes, lentils and tomatoes

4. Bring to a boil, then reduce the heat and simmer for at least 30 minutes

5. Pulse using a blender

6. Serve immediately

BROCCOLI AND RED CAPSICUM SOUP

Serves: **4**

Prep Time: **10** Minutes

Cook Time: **15** Minutes

Total Time: **25** Minutes

INGREDIENTS

- 1 cup broccoli florets
- 1 cup red capsicum
- 1 tsp oil
- 1 tablespoon garlic
- ¼ cup onions
- pinch of salt
- 1 tsp pepper powder

DIRECTIONS

1. In a pan sauté onions and garlic for 2-3 minutes
2. Add salt, red capsicum, broccoli, 1 cup water, and mix well
3. Cover with a lid cook for 5-6 minutes
4. When ready remove from heat and blend using a mixer
5. Transfer the mixture back to the pan, add ¼ cup water, pepper powder and cook for another 2-3 minutes
6. When ready remove from heat and serve

CANTALOUPE SOUP

Serves: **4**

Prep Time: **10**   Minutes

Cook Time: **15**   Minutes

Total Time: **25**   Minutes

INGREDIENTS

- 2 cantaloupes
- 1 tsp ginger
- ½ tsp nutmeg
- ½ cup fat-free sour cream

DIRECTIONS

1. Remove seeds from cantaloupes and refrigerate
2. Pour melon into a blender with spices, sour cream and blend until smooth
3. Refrigerate for another hour and pour soup into the bowl
4. Garnish with nutmeg, ginger and serve

GREEN PESTO PASTA

Serves: 2

Prep Time: 5   Minutes

Cook Time: 15   Minutes

Total Time: 20   Minutes

INGREDIENTS

- 4 oz. spaghetti
- 2 cups basil leaves
- 2 garlic cloves
- ¼ cup olive oil
- 2 tablespoons parmesan cheese
- ½ tsp black pepper

DIRECTIONS

1. Bring water to a boil and add pasta
2. In a blend add parmesan cheese, basil leaves, garlic and blend
3. Add olive oil, pepper and blend again
4. Pour pesto onto pasta and serve when ready

BUCKWHEAT DOSA

Serves: **4**

Prep Time: **5** Minutes

Cook Time: **20** Minutes

Total Time: **25** Minutes

INGREDIENTS

- 1 cup buckwheat
- 1 tablespoon olive oil
- 1 tsp mustard seeds
- ½ tsp asafetida
- 1 tsp green chilies
- 1 tablespoon coriander
- 1 tablespoon urad dal

DIRECTIONS

1. In a bowl combine urad dal and buckwheat, using a mixer blend until smooth
2. In a pan add mustard seeds, asafetida, chilies, salt, coriander, water, and mix well
3. Pour 1/3 cup batter in a circular manner and cook until golden brown
4. When ready remove and serve

Serves: **3**

Prep Time: **10** Minutes

Cook Time: **30** Minutes

Total Time: **40** Minutes

INGREDIENTS

- ½ cup zucchini
- ¼ cup bajra
- 1 tsp olive oil
- 1 tsp cumin seeds
- ¼ cup red capsicum
- ¼ cup green capsicum
- ¼ cup almond milk
- ¼ tsp chili paste
- ¼ cup coriander

DIRECTIONS

1. Soak the bajra in water overnight
2. In a pressure cooker combine water, bajra and mix well
3. Allow the steam to go away before opening the lid
4. In a pan add cumin seeds, asafetida and sauté for 1-2 minutes
5. Add capsicum, zucchini, salt and sauté for another 3-4 minutes

6. Add milk, coriander, chili paste and cook for another 2-3 minutes
7. When ready remove from heat and serve

QUINOA MUTHIA

Serves: *5*

Prep Time: *10*   Minutes

Cook Time: *40*   Minutes

Total Time: *50*   Minutes

INGREDIENTS

- ½ cup quinoa flour
- 1 cup besan
- ¼ cup semolina
- 1 cup bottle gourd
- 6 tsp oil
- 2 tsp chilli paste
- 1 pinch baking soda
- ¼ tsp asafetida
- ¼ tsp turmeric powder
- 1 tsp lemon juice
- 1 tsp mustard seeds
- 1 tsp sesame seeds
- 3 curry leaves
- 1 tablespoon coriander

DIRECTIONS

1. In a bowl combine semolina, besan, quinoa flour, 1 tsp oil, chili paste, gourd, asafetida, turmeric powder, lemon juice, and salt
2. Divide mixture into 4-5 portions and shape them into patties
3. Steam in a steamer for 10-15 minutes
4. When ready, remove from the steamer
5. In a pan add remaining oil, sesame seeds, curry leaves, asafetida and sauté for 1 minute
6. Add muthia, sauté for 2-3 minutes and serve with coriander

LIME GRILLED CORN

Serves: *3*

Prep Time: *5*   Minutes

Cook Time: *15*   Minutes

Total Time: *20*   Minutes

INGREDIENTS

- 3 ears of corn
- 2 tablespoons mayonnaise
- 2 tablespoons squeezed lime juice
- ½ tsp chili powder
- 1 pinch of salt

DIRECTIONS

1. Place corn onto the grill and cook for 5-6 minutes or until the kernels being to brown
2. Turn every few minutes until all sides are slightly charred
3. In a bowl mix the rest of ingredients
4. Spread a light coating of the mixture onto each corn and serve

CAPSICUM AND PANEER SUBZI

Serves: **5**

Prep Time: **10** Minutes

Cook Time: **15** Minutes

Total Time: **25** Minutes

INGREDIENTS

- 2 cups capsicum cubes
- ¼ cup paneer
- 1 tsp oil
- ¼ cup onion cubes
- ¼ tsp ginger paste
- 1 tsp garlic paste
- 1 tsp dried fenugreek leaves
- 1 cup tomato pulp
- ¼ tsp turmeric powder
- ¼ tsp chili powder
- 1 tsp garam masala
- pinch of salt

DIRECTIONS

1. In a pan sauté onion
2. Add garlic paste, fenugreek leaves, ginger paste and sauté for 1 minute

3. Add capsicum, turmeric powder, tomato pulp, chili powder, garam masala and mix well

4. Cook for 5-6 minutes, add salt, paneer and mix well

5. Cook for another 2-3 minutes, when ready remove from heat and serve

AVOCADO DIP

Serves: **4**

Prep Time: **5**   Minutes

Cook Time: **5**   Minutes

Total Time: **10**   Minutes

INGREDIENTS

- 1 cup mashed avocado
- 1 tsp lemon juice
- 1 tablespoon tomatoes
- ¼ tsp green chilies
- pinch of salt

DIRECTIONS

1. In a bowl combine all ingredients together and mix well
2. When ready serve with corn chips

ONION PURIS

Serves: *28*

Prep Time: *5*   Minutes

Cook Time: *20*   Minutes

Total Time: *25*   Minutes

INGREDIENTS

- ½ cup jowar
- ½ cup onions
- 1 tsp sesame seeds
- pinch of salt
- ¼ tsp oil

DIRECTIONS

1. In a bowl combine all ingredients together
2. Divide dough into 22-28 portions
3. Press each portion of dough between your hands until it looks like a thin circle
4. Grease a baking tray with oil
5. Bake for 18-20 minutes at 350 F
6. When ready remove and serve

Serves: **6**

Prep Time: **10** Minutes

Cook Time: **25** Minutes

Total Time: **35** Minutes

INGREDIENTS

- 1 bunch of kale
- 1 tablespoon olive oil
- 1 tsp salt

DIRECTIONS

1. Preheat the oven to 325 F
2. Chop the kale into chip size pieces
3. Put pieces into a bowl tops with olive oil and salt
4. Spread the leaves in a single layer onto a parchment paper
5. Bake for 20-25 minutes
6. When ready, remove and serve

CRANBERRY SALAD

Serves: 2

Prep Time: 5   Minutes

Cook Time: 5   Minutes

Total Time: 10   Minutes

INGREDIENTS

- 1 can unsweetened pineapple
- 1 package cherry gelatin
- 1 tablespoon lemon juice
- ½ cup artificial sweetener
- 1 cup cranberries
- 1 orange
- 1 cup celery
- ½ cup pecans

DIRECTIONS

1. In a bowl mix all ingredients and mix well
2. Serve with dressing

Serves: **2**

Prep Time: **5**   Minutes

Cook Time: **5**   Minutes

Total Time: ***10***   Minutes

INGREDIENTS

- 8 oz. romaine lettuce
- 2 cups radicchio
- ¼ red onion
- 2 ribs celery
- 1 cup tomatoes
- 1 can chickpeas
- 1 cup salad dressing

DIRECTIONS

1. In a bowl mix all ingredients and mix well
2. Serve with dressing

CHICKPEA COLESLAW

Serves: **2**

Prep Time: **5** Minutes

Cook Time: **5** Minutes

Total Time: **10** Minutes

INGREDIENTS

- 2 cans chickpeas
- 2 cups carrots
- 1 cup celery
- ¼ cup green onions
- ¼ cup dill leaves
- ¼ cup olive oil
- 1 cucumber
- 1 cup salad dressing

DIRECTIONS

1. In a bowl mix all ingredients and mix well
2. Serve with dressing

ROMAINE SALAD

Serves: **2**

Prep Time: **5** Minutes

Cook Time: **5** Minutes

Total Time: **10** Minutes

INGREDIENTS

- 1 cup cooked quinoa
- 1 cup sunflower seeds
- 1 tablespoon olive oil
- 1 head romaine lettuce
- 1 cup carrots
- 1 cup cabbage
- ¼ cup radishes

DIRECTIONS

1. In a bowl mix all ingredients and mix well
2. Serve with dressing

Serves: **2**

Prep Time: **5**   Minutes

Cook Time: **5**   Minutes

Total Time: **10**   Minutes

INGREDIENTS

- 1 bunch coriander leaves
- 1 bunch mint leaves
- ¼ red onion
- 1 bunch parsley
- 1 cup lentils
- 1 tablespoon pumpkin seeds
- 1 tablespoon pine nuts

DIRECTIONS

1. **In a bowl mix all ingredients and mix well**
2. **Serve with dressing**

QUINOA SALAD

Serves: **2**

Prep Time: **5**   Minutes

Cook Time: **5**   Minutes

Total Time: ***10***   Minutes

INGREDIENTS

- 1 cauliflower
- 2 cups cooked quinoa
- 1 can chickpeas
- 1 cup baby spinach
- ¼ cup parsley
- ¼ cup cilantro
- ¼ cup green onion
- ½ cup feta cheese

DIRECTIONS

1. In a bowl mix all ingredients and mix well
2. Serve with dressing

Serves: **2**

Prep Time: **5**   Minutes

Cook Time: **5**   Minutes

Total Time: **10** Minutes

INGREDIENTS

- 1 head romaine lettuce
- 1 cup tomatoes
- 1 cup cucumber
- 1 cup celery
- ¼ cup olives
- 1 shallot
- 1 cup salad dressing

DIRECTIONS

1. **In a bowl mix all ingredients and mix well**
2. **Serve with dressing**

COUSCOUS SALAD

Serves: **2**

Prep Time: **5**   Minutes

Cook Time: **5**   Minutes

Total Time: **10**   Minutes

INGREDIENTS

- 1 cup couscous
- ¼ cup pine nuts
- ¼ cup olive lil
- 1 tablespoon lemon juice
- 1 shallot
- 2 cloves garlic
- 1 tsp salt
- 1 can chickpeas
- 1 cup tomatoes
- ½ cup feta cheese
- 1 zucchini
- 1 tablespoon basil

DIRECTIONS

1. In a bowl mix all ingredients and mix well
2. Serve with dressing

Serves: **2**
Prep Time: **5**   Minutes

Cook Time: **5**   Minutes

Total Time: **10**   Minutes

INGREDIENTS

- 1 cup cooked FARRO
- 1 bay leaf
- 1 shallot
- ¼ cup olive oil
- 2 cups arugula
- ¼ cup parmesan cheese
- ¼ cup basil
- ¼ cup parsley
- ¼ cup pecans

DIRECTIONS

1. In a bowl mix all ingredients and mix well
2. Serve with dressing

Serves: **2**

Prep Time: **5**   Minutes

Cook Time: **5**   Minutes

Total Time: **10**   Minutes

INGREDIENTS

- 1 head leaf lettuce
- 1 red bell pepper
- 2 mangoes
- ¼ green onion
- ¼ cup peanuts
- ¼ cup cilantro
- 1 cup peanut dressing

DIRECTIONS

1. In a bowl mix all ingredients and mix well
2. Serve with dressing

LENTIL FRITATTA

Serves: **2**
Prep Time: **10**   Minutes

Cook Time: **20**   Minutes

Total Time: **30**   Minutes

INGREDIENTS

- ½ lb. lentil
- 1 tablespoon olive oil
- ½ red onion
- ¼ tsp salt
- 2 eggs
- 2 oz. cheddar cheese
- 1 garlic clove
- ¼ tsp dill

DIRECTIONS

1. In a bowl whisk eggs with salt and cheese
2. In a frying pan heat olive oil and pour egg mixture
3. Add remaining ingredients and mix well
4. Serve when ready

SPINACH FRITATTA

Serves: **2**

Prep Time: **10** Minutes

Cook Time: **20** Minutes

Total Time: **30** Minutes

INGREDIENTS

- ½ lb. spinach
- 1 tablespoon olive oil
- ½ red onion
- 2 eggs
- ¼ tsp salt
- 2 oz. cheddar cheese
- 1 garlic clove
- ¼ tsp dill

DIRECTIONS

1. In a skillet sauté spinach until tender
2. In a bowl whisk eggs with salt and cheese
3. In a frying pan heat olive oil and pour egg mixture
4. Add remaining ingredients and mix well
5. When ready serve with sautéed spinach

Serves: **2**

Prep Time: **10** Minutes

Cook Time: **20** Minutes

Total Time: **30** Minutes

INGREDIENTS

- 1 cup cooked black beans
- 1 tablespoon olive oil
- ½ red onion
- ¼ tsp salt
- 2 oz. cheddar cheese
- 1 garlic clove
- ¼ tsp dill
- 2 eggs

DIRECTIONS

1. In a bowl whisk eggs with salt and cheese
2. In a frying pan heat olive oil and pour egg mixture
3. Add remaining ingredients and mix well
4. Serve when ready

CHEESE FRITATTA

Serves: **2**

Prep Time: **10** Minutes

Cook Time: **20** Minutes

Total Time: **30** Minutes

INGREDIENTS

- 1 tablespoon olive oil
- ½ red onion
- ¼ tsp salt
- 2 oz. cheddar cheese
- 1 garlic clove
- ¼ tsp dill
- 2 eggs

DIRECTIONS

1. In a bowl combine cheddar cheese and onion
2. In a frying pan heat olive oil and pour egg mixture
3. Add remaining ingredients and mix well
4. Serve when ready

BROCCOLI FRITATTA

Serves: *2*

Prep Time: *10* Minutes

Cook Time: *20* Minutes

Total Time: *30* Minutes

INGREDIENTS

- 1 cup broccoli
- 1 tablespoon olive oil
- ½ red onion
- ¼ tsp salt
- 2 oz. cheddar cheese
- 1 garlic clove
- 2 eggs
- ¼ tsp dill

DIRECTIONS

1. In a skillet sauté broccoli until tender
2. In a bowl whisk eggs with salt and cheese
3. In a frying pan heat olive oil and pour egg mixture
4. Add remaining ingredients and mix well
5. When ready serve with sautéed broccoli

SHAKSHUKA

Serves: **2**
Prep Time: **10** Minutes

Cook Time: **20** Minutes

Total Time: **30** Minutes

INGREDIENTS

- 1 tablespoon olive oil
- 1 red onion
- 1 red chili
- 1 garlic clove
- 2 cans cherry tomatoes
- 2 eggs

DIRECTIONS

1. In a frying pan cook garlic, chili, onions until soft
2. Stir in tomatoes and cook until mixture thickens
3. Crack the eggs over the sauce
4. Cover with a lid and cook for another 7-8 minutes
5. When ready remove from heat and serve

BROCCOLI CASSEROLE

Serves: **4**

Prep Time: **10**   Minutes

Cook Time: **15**   Minutes

Total Time: **25**   Minutes

INGREDIENTS

- 1 onion
- 2 chicken breasts
- 2 tablespoons unsalted butter
- 2 eggs
- 2 cups cooked rice
- 2 cups cheese
- 1 cup parmesan cheese
- 2 cups cooked broccoli

DIRECTIONS

1. Sauté the veggies and set aside
2. Preheat the oven to 425 F
3. Transfer the sautéed veggies to a baking dish, add remaining ingredients to the baking dish
4. Mix well, add seasoning and place the dish in the oven
5. Bake for 12-15 minutes or until slightly brown
6. When ready remove from the oven and serve

BEAN FRITATTA

Serves: *2*

Prep Time: *10*   Minutes

Cook Time: *20*   Minutes

Total Time: *30*   Minutes

INGREDIENTS

- 1 cup black beans
- 1 tablespoon olive oil
- ½ red onion
- 2 eggs
- ¼ tsp salt
- 2 oz. cheddar cheese
- 1 garlic clove
- ¼ tsp dill

DIRECTIONS

1. In a bowl whisk eggs with salt and cheese
2. In a frying pan heat olive oil and pour egg mixture
3. Add remaining ingredients and mix well
4. Serve when ready

Serves: **3-4**

Prep Time: **10**   Minutes

Cook Time: **20**   Minutes

Total Time: **30**   Minutes

INGREDIENTS

- 2 delicata squashes
- 2 tablespoons olive oil
- 1 tsp curry powder
- 1 tsp salt

DIRECTIONS

1. Preheat the oven to 400 F
2. Cut everything in half lengthwise
3. Toss everything with olive oil and place onto a prepared baking sheet
4. Roast for 18-20 minutes at 400 F or until golden brown
5. When ready remove from the oven and serve

Serves: **2**

Prep Time: **10** Minutes

Cook Time: **20** Minutes

Total Time: **30** Minutes

INGREDIENTS

- 1 lb. sweet. potatoes
- 2 tablespoons olive oil
- 1 tablespoon smoked paprika
- 1 tablespoon salt

DIRECTIONS

1. Preheat the oven to 425 F
2. In a bowl toss everything with olive oil and seasoning
3. Spread everything onto a prepared baking sheet
4. Bake for 8-10 minutes or until crisp
5. When ready remove from the oven and serve

ZUCCHINI CHIPS

Serves: 2

Prep Time: *10*   Minutes

Cook Time: *20*   Minutes

Total Time: *30*   Minutes

INGREDIENTS

- 1 lb. zucchini
- 2 tablespoons olive oil
- 1 tablespoon smoked paprika
- 1 tablespoon salt

DIRECTIONS

1. Preheat the oven to 425 F
2. In a bowl toss everything with olive oil and seasoning
3. Spread everything onto a prepared baking sheet
4. Bake for 8-10 minutes or until crisp
5. When ready remove from the oven and serve

PIZZA RECIPES

ZUCCHINI PIZZA CRUST

Serves: **4**

Prep Time: **10**   Minutes

Cook Time: **30**   Minutes

Total Time: **40**   Minutes

INGREDIENTS

- 4 zucchinis
- 2 tsp salt
- 2 cups almond flour
- 2 tablespoons coconut flour
- 3 eggs
- 2 ½ cups cheddar cheese
- 1 tsp red pepper flakes
- 1 tsp dried oregano

DIRECTIONS

1. Shred the zucchini, sprinkle with salt and set aside
2. Preheat the oven to 400 F
3. Mix zucchini with remaining ingredients
4. Place the dough over a baking sheet and spread evenly

5. Pop the pizza crust in the oven for 30 minutes or until golden brown

6. When ready, remove and serve

BARBEQUE PIZZA

Serves: **2**

Prep Time: **10**   Minutes

Cook Time: **15**   Minutes

Total Time: **25**   Minutes

INGREDIENTS

- 1 pizza crust
- 1 tsp olive oil
- 1 cup onion
- ¼ cup red pepper strips
- 1 cup cooked chicken
- ¼ cup barbecue sauce
- 1 cup mozzarella cheese

DIRECTIONS

1. In a frying pan add pepper strips, onion and fry until soft
2. Add barbecue sauce, chicken and stir well
3. On a ready-made pizza crust spread onion, pepper mix, chicken and top with mozzarella
4. Bake for 12-15 minutes at 425 F

SHRIMP PIZZA

Serves: *4*

Prep Time: 5   Minutes

Cook Time: *20*   Minutes

Total Time: 25   Minutes

INGREDIENTS

- 1 package pizza dough
- 1 tablespoon cornmeal
- 1/3 cup ricotta cheese
- 1 lb. shrimp
- 5 cloves roasted garlic
- 2 ¼ cups mozzarella cheese
- 1 tablespoon basil

DIRECTIONS

1. Stretch pizza dough across a baking pan and bake for 6-8 minutes, sprinkle cornmeal over the pan
2. Mix ricotta cheese, garlic, shrimp together and place over pizza crust
3. Cover pizza with mozzarella and basil
4. Bake for 12-15 minutes at 425 F

CAULIFLOWER CRUST PIZZA

Serves: **4**

Prep Time: **10**   Minutes

Cook Time: **20**   Minutes

Total Time: **30**   Minutes

INGREDIENTS

- 1 lb. ground beef
- 1 egg
- 1 tsp parsley
- 1 tsp dried basil
- ¼ tsp salt
- ½ tsp pepper
- ¼ cup tomato puree
- 1 tsp tomato paste
- ¼ red pepper
- 1 tsp dried basil
- ¼ cup olives
- 5 slices prosciutto
- 4 oz. parmesan
- 1 handful fresh basil

DIRECTIONS

1. Preheat the oven to 430 F
2. In a bowl add salt, mince, egg, basil, pepper, parsley and mix well
3.   Roll into a ball and place on a baking tray
4. Bake for 12-15 minutes
5. Mix the tomato paste with tomato puree and spread across the base
6. Top with peppers, prosciutto, parmesan, olives and bake for another 8-10 minutes
7. Remove from the oven, top with basil leaves and serve

THIRD COOKBOOK

ROAST RECIPES

ROASTED ONION

Serves: **3-4**

Prep Time: **10** Minutes

Cook Time: **20** Minutes

Total Time: **30** Minutes

INGREDIENTS

- 1 lb. onion
- 2 tablespoons olive oil
- 1 tsp curry powder
- 1 tsp salt

DIRECTIONS

1. Preheat the oven to 400 F
2. Cut everything in half lengthwise
3. Toss everything with olive oil and place onto a prepared baking sheet
4. Roast for 18-20 minutes at 400 F or until golden brown
5. When ready remove from the oven and serve

ROASTED SQUASH

Serves: **3-4**
Prep Time: **10**   Minutes

Cook Time: **20**   Minutes

Total Time: **30**   Minutes

INGREDIENTS

- 2 delicata squashes
- 2 tablespoons olive oil
- 1 tsp curry powder
- 1 tsp salt

DIRECTIONS

1. Preheat the oven to 400 F
2. Cut everything in half lengthwise
3. Toss everything with olive oil and place onto a prepared baking sheet
4. Roast for 18-20 minutes at 400 F or until golden brown
5. When ready remove from the oven and serve

ROASTED GARLIC

Serves: 2

Prep Time: **10**   Minutes

Cook Time: **10**   Minutes

Total Time: **20**   Minutes

INGREDIENTS

- 1 head garlic
- 1 tablespoon olive oil

DIRECTIONS

1. Preheat oven to 375 F
2. Ove the garlic drizzle the olive oil and add to the pan
3. Roast for 15-20 minutes and remove from the oven
4. Let it cool and serve

SOUP RECIPES

ZUCCHINI SOUP

Serves: **4**

Prep Time: **10** Minutes

Cook Time: **20** Minutes

Total Time: **30** Minutes

INGREDIENTS

- 1 tablespoon olive oil
- 1 lb. zucchini
- ¼ red onion
- ½ cup all-purpose flour
- ¼ tsp salt
- ¼ tsp pepper
- 1 can vegetable broth
- 1 cup heavy cream

DIRECTIONS

1. In a saucepan heat olive oil and sauté zucchini until tender
2. Add remaining ingredients to the saucepan and bring to a boil
3. When all the vegetables are tender transfer to a blender and blend until smooth
4. Pour soup into bowls, garnish with parsley and serve

Serves: *3*

Prep Time: *10*   Minutes

Cook Time: *50*   Minutes

Total Time: *60*   Minutes

INGREDIENTS

- 1 head cauliflower
- 1 apple
- 1 tablespoon olive oil
- 2 cups almond milk
- 1 tablespoon fresh basil
- 1 tsp curry powder
- 1 tsp sesame seeds

DIRECTIONS

1. Preheat oven to 350 F and place the cauliflower on a prepared baking sheet
2. Drizzle with salt, pepper and olive oil
3. Roast for 40-45 minutes and remove from the oven
4. In a blender mix the cauliflower with the rest of the ingredients until smooth
5. Season with sesame seeds and serve

SWEET POTATO SOUP

Serves: **3**

Prep Time: **10** Minutes

Cook Time: **50** Minutes

Total Time: **60** Minutes

INGREDIENTS

- 1 sweet potato
- 1 tsp olive oil
- 1 lbs. cranberries
- ½ cup water
- 1 tablespoon cashew butter
- 1 tsp salt

DIRECTIONS

1. Preheat oven to 350 F and place the potatoes on a baking sheet, rub them with olive oil and roast for 45-50 minutes
2. Meanwhile cook the cranberries until tender, remove from the heat when ready
3. Remove the sweet potato from the oven and place blend it in a blender with cranberries and cashew butter and salt
4. Pour in a bowl and serve

GREEN PESTO PASTA

Serves: **2**

Prep Time: **5** Minutes

Cook Time: **15** Minutes

Total Time: **20** Minutes

INGREDIENTS

- 4 oz. spaghetti
- 2 cups basil leaves
- 2 garlic cloves
- ¼ cup olive oil
- 2 tablespoons parmesan cheese
- ½ tsp black pepper

DIRECTIONS

1. Bring water to a boil and add pasta
2. In a blend add parmesan cheese, basil leaves, garlic and blend
3. Add olive oil, pepper and blend again
4. Pour pesto onto pasta and serve when ready

FAJITA LETTUCE WRAPS

Serves: **2**
Prep Time: **10**   Minutes

Cook Time: **10**   Minutes

Total Time: **20**   Minutes

INGREDIENTS

- 2 tablespoons olive oil
- 1 onion
- ¼ cumin
- ¼ cup tomatoes
- 1 tablespoon walnuts
- 2 tablespoons parsley
- 3 carrots
- 1 zucchini
- ¼ tsp salt
- ¼ tsp pepper
- ¼ tsp cinnamon

DIRECTIONS

1. In a skillet sauté the olive oil and onion over low heat
2. Add carrots and zucchini and cook for 5-6 minutes
3. Add cinnamon, pepper and salt and cook for 1-2 minutes

4. Spoon into lettuce leaves and add walnuts, parsley and tomatoes

FAJITAS WITH BASIL SAUCE

Serves: **2**

Prep Time: **10**   Minutes

Cook Time: **20**   Minutes

Total Time: **30**   Minutes

INGREDIENTS

- ½ cup quinoa
- 1 cup water
- ½ cup onion
- 1 tablespoon parsley
- 1 tsp lemon zest
- 6 tortillas
- 1 can cannellini beans
- 1 pint cheery tomatoes
- 1 cucumber

Basil sauce
- 8 tomatillos
- 2 tablespoons cannellini beans
- 1 cucumber
- 1 tablespoon almond butter
- 3 basil leaves

DIRECTIONS

1. Hold tortilla over flame to low heat for 3-4 seconds each side
2. Cook quinoa for 10-15 minutes and remove form heat
3. Puree the basil sauce ingredients in a blender
4. Season with salt and pepper and serve

BRUSEELS SPROUTS WITH BALSAMIC GLAZE

Serves: **3**

Prep Time: **10**   Minutes

Cook Time: **40**   Minutes

Total Time: **50**   Minutes

INGREDIENTS

- 1 head garlic
- 1 lbs. Brussels sprouts
- 1 tablespoon olive oil
- 1 kale
- ½ cup cabbage
- 1 tablespoon almonds
- 1 tsp lemon zest
- 1 tablespoon cherries

Balsamic Glaze
- ½ cup tahini
- 1 tablespoon balsamic vinegar
- 1 tablespoon lemon juice
- salt
- pepper

DIRECTIONS

1. Preheat oven to 375 F and place a baking sheet with parchment paper
2. Slice the garlic and drizzle it and Brussels sprouts with oil, salt and pepper
3. Place them on the baking sheet and roast for 25-30 minutes, remove them when ready
4. Drizzle with balsamic glaze (mix all the ingredients in a bowl)

ROASTED SWEET POTATOES

Serves: **4**

Prep Time: **10** Minutes

Cook Time: **50** Minutes

Total Time: **60** Minutes

INGREDIENTS

- 2 sweet potatoes
- 1 tsp olive oil

Sauce

- ½ avocado diced
- ¼ peach halves
- 3 basil leaves
- 1 tablespoon red onion
- 2 tablespoons water
- ¼ navel orange juiced

DIRECTIONS

1. Preheat the oven to 375 F and place the sweet potatoes on a baking sheet
2. Rub them with olive oil and roast for 40-45 minutes and remove from oven when ready
3. For sauce combine all the ingredients in a blender

SPAGHETTI SQUASH PLATTER

Serves: **3**

Prep Time: **10** Minutes

Cook Time: **40** Minutes

Total Time: **50** Minutes

INGREDIENTS

- 1 spaghetti squash
- 1 tablespoon onion
- 1 avocado peeled
- 1 whole pear
- 1 tablespoon cashews
- 1 tablespoon nuts
- 1 tablespoon cherries
- 1 tablespoon fresh dill
- 1 tsp sesame seeds
- 1 tablespoon olive oil
- 1 cucumber

Tahini Garlic Dressing

- ½ cup tahini
- 1 clove garlic
- ¼ cup water

DIRECTIONS

1. Preheat oven to 350 F and place squash on a baking sheet and drizzle with olive oil and salt

2. Roast for 40-45 minutes and remove from oven when ready

3. Scoop out the spaghetti squash except the sesame seeds and dill

4. Mix all the ingredients in a bowl and drizzle over the squash and sprinkle with the dill

Serves: **4**

Prep Time: **10** Minutes

Cook Time: **30** Minutes

Total Time: **40** Minutes

INGREDIENTS

- 1 large head cauliflower
- 1 red pepper
- 2 tablespoons red onion
- 1 tablespoon macadamia nuts
- 1 scallion
- 1 fresh basil leave
- 1 can sardines
- 1 tablespoon olive oil
- ½ cup wild rice

DIRECTIONS

1. Preheat oven to 375 F and line a baking sheet
2. Place the cauliflower on the baking sheet and drizzle with olive oil and salt
3. Roast for 20-25 minutes and remove when ready
4. Cook the rice and place it on a platter and add the cauliflower, season with salt and serve

SALAD WITH KALE CAULIFLOWER

Serves: **2**

Prep Time: **10**   Minutes

Cook Time: **20**   Minutes

Total Time: **30**   Minutes

INGREDIENTS

- 1 head cauliflower
- 1 cup arugula
- 1 tablespoon sunflower seeds
- ¼ cup tahini
- 1 garlic clove
- 1 tablespoon olive oil
- 1 head purple kale
- 1 cup cherry tomatoes
- 1 head cabbage
- 1 cup green grapes

DIRECTIONS

1. Preheat the oven to 375 F and place the cauliflower on a baking sheet and drizzle with olive oil and salt
2. Roast for 20-25 minutes and remove when ready
3. In a bowl combine cabbage, grapes, arugula, sunflower seeds, kale and tomatoes

4. In bowl mix tahini and garlic clove and drizzle over the salad

Serves: **3**

Prep Time: **10** Minutes

Cook Time: **10** Minutes

Total Time: **20** Minutes

INGREDIENTS

- 1 tablespoon avocado oil
- 3 carrots
- 3 large nori sheets
- 1 tomato
- 1 tablespoon fresh cilantro
- 1 red pepper
- 1 green bell pepper
- 1 while onion
- 1 jalapeno

DIRECTIONS

1. In a skillet sauce avocado oil, onion, jalapeno, white onion, salt and pepper for 6-7 minutes
2. Remove from heat and place mixture in a bowl
3. Sauté carrots with pepper and salt for 5-6 minutes
4. Combine coconut milk with curry powder and combine with red onion, sea s alt and pepper

5. Lay the nori sheets and top with pepper mixture and carrots and drizzle with coconut milk

LIME SPINACH CHIPS

Serves: **6**
Prep Time: **10**   Minutes

Cook Time: **30**   Minutes

Total Time: **40**   Minutes

INGREDIENTS

-   1 whole lime
-   ¼ tsp salt
-   6 cups spinach
-   2 tablespoons olive oil

DIRECTIONS

1. In a bowl toss the spinach with olive oil and lime juice
2. Add salt, and distribute the spinach evenly onto a cookie sheet
3. Bake for 30 minutes at 300 F
4. When ready remove from the oven and serve

AIP BREADSTICKS

Serves: **6-8**
Prep Time: **10**   Minutes

Cook Time: **15**   Minutes

Total Time: **25**   Minutes

INGREDIENTS

- 4 tablespoons olive oil
- 2 tablespoons water
- ½ cup coconut flour
- ¼ tsp baking soda
- 1 tsp rosemary
- 1 tsp lemon juice
- 1 tablespoon unflavored gelatin
- ¼ tsp garlic powder
- ¼ tsp salt

DIRECTIONS

1. Preheat oven to 325 F
2. In a blender add gelatin, 1 tablespoon of water, and blend
3. Add the rest of ingredients and blend until it thickens
4. Remove dough and divide into 6-8 portions
5. Grease each ball with olive oil and form small sticks

6. Sprinkle garlic, salt and rosemary on each one

7. Bake at 325 F for 12-15 minutes

8. When ready remove from the oven and serve

CAULIFLOWER RICE

Serves: **4**

Prep Time: **10** Minutes

Cook Time: **15** Minutes

Total Time: **25** Minutes

INGREDIENTS

- 1 clove garlic
- 1 tablespoon olive oil
- 1 head cauliflower
- ¼ cup yellow onion
- ¼ tsp salt
- 1 tsp herb seasoning

DIRECTIONS

1. Grate the cauliflower and place it in a blender
2. Blend until smooth
3. In a skillet heat coconut oil
4. Sauté garlic, onion and cauliflower for 4-5 minutes
5. Season with salt, pepper and serve

GLAZED SALMON

Serves: **2**

Prep Time: **10** Minutes

Cook Time: **25** Minutes

Total Time: **35** Minutes

INGREDIENTS

- 12 oz. salmon filet
- 1 tablespoon maple syrup
- 1 tablespoon coconut aminos
- 1 tablespoon olive oil

DIRECTIONS

1. Preheat the oven to 325 F
2. In a saucepan add maple syrup, coconut aminos and olive oil and stir until a glaze has formed
3. Place salmon filet on a baking sheet and brush with glaze
4. Bake for 20-25 minutes or until the fish is tender
5. When ready remove from heat and serve

BISON STEW

Serves: *6*

Prep Time: *10*   Minutes

Cook Time: *50*   Minutes

Total Time: *60*   Minutes

INGREDIENTS

- 2 lb. bison steak
- 1 tablespoon coconut oil
- 2 cups celery
- 2 sprig thyme
- 1 head cauliflower
- 1 onion
- 1-quart beef broth
- ¼ tsp salt

DIRECTIONS

1. In a skillet brown the stew on both sides and transfer to a pot
2. In the pot add celery, onion and beef broth
3. Add celery, thyme, cauliflower and bring to a boil
4. Simmer for 40-50 minutes or until the stew is completely cooked

GARLIC AND HERB SCALLOPS

Serves: **4**

Prep Time: **10**   Minutes

Cook Time: **15**   Minutes

Total Time: **25**   Minutes

INGREDIENTS

- ¼ cup water
- 1 tablespoon olive oil
- 1 tablespoon lemon juice
- ¼ tsp salt
- ¼ tsp onion powder
- ¼ tsp garlic
- 4 oz. scallops
- 1 cup kale
- 1 tablespoon salad dressing

DIRECTIONS

1. In a pot toss scallop with salad dressing
2. Place scallops in a steamer with all vegetables and steam for 12-15 minutes
3. Remove from pot and place vegetables on a plate
4. Add lemon juice, seasoning and serve

ROASTED ROSEMARY BEETS

Serves: **2**

Prep Time: **10** Minutes

Cook Time: **35** Minutes

Total Time: **45** Minutes

INGREDIENTS

- 2 tablespoons olive oil
- 2 tablespoons rosemary
- 2 beets
- ¼ salt

DIRECTIONS

1. Preheat the oven to 375 F
2. Brush beets with olive oil, sprinkle with salt and rosemary
3. Place the beets in a baking dish
4. Roast beets for 30-35 minutes
5. When ready remove from the oven and serve

BACON-WRAPPED SHRIMP

Serves: *8*
Prep Time: *10* Minutes

Cook Time: *30* Minutes

Total Time: *40* Minutes

INGREDIENTS

- 1 lb. shrimp
- 12 oz. bacon

DIRECTIONS

1. Cut bacon in half and wrap each shrimp with bacon
2. Skewer each shrimp and place the skewers on a baking sheet
3. Cook for 25-30 minutes
4. When ready remove from the oven and serve

Serves: **4**

Prep Time: **10** Minutes

Cook Time: **20** Minutes

Total Time: **30** Minutes

INGREDIENTS

- 2 tablespoons lard
- 1 lb. pork chops
- ¼ onion
- 1 tsp fennel
- ¼ tsp salt
- Juice of 1 lemon

DIRECTIONS

1. In a skillet add the onions and cook until soft
2. Season pork chops with salt and fennel
3. Place the pork chops in the skillet and cook for 5-6 minutes per side
4. Remove pork chops from the pan and set aside
5. Add lemon juice, parsley and pour mixture over pork chops, serve when ready

Serves: **4**

Prep Time: **5**   Minutes

Cook Time: **10**   Minutes

Total Time: **15**   Minutes

INGREDIENTS

- 1 bunch kale
- 2 oz. bacon
- ½ cup broth
- 1 tablespoon lemon juice
- 1 clove garlic

DIRECTIONS

1. Place the bacon in a skillet and cook until crispy
2. Add broth, kale, and cook until broth has evaporated
3. Add garlic, lemon juice and stir for 1-2 minutes
4. When ready remove and serve

Serves: 2

Prep Time: 5   Minutes

Cook Time: 5   Minutes

Total Time: **10**   Minutes

INGREDIENTS

- 1 cup cherry tomatoes
- 1 cucumber
- 1 cup olives
- ½ cup onion
- 1 cup feta
- 1 cup salad dressing

DIRECTIONS

1. In a bowl mix all ingredients and mix well
2. Serve with dressing

Serves: **2**
Prep Time: **5**   Minutes
Cook Time: **5**   Minutes
Total Time: **10** Minutes

INGREDIENTS

- 1 cup cooked lentils
- 1 tsp salt
- 1 cup cooked quinoa
- 2 tablespoons olive oil
- 1 tsp salt
- 1 tomato
- 1 avocado
- 1 tsp cilantro

DIRECTIONS

1. **In a bowl mix all ingredients and mix well**
2. **Serve with dressing**

Serves: 2
Prep Time: 5   Minutes
Cook Time: 5   Minutes
Total Time: **10**   Minutes

INGREDIENTS

- 2 cups cooked quinoa
- 1 cup spinach leaves
- ¼ cup cranberries
- ¼ cup walnuts
- ½ avocado

DIRECTIONS

1. In a bowl mix all ingredients and mix well
2. Serve with dressing

Serves: **2**
Prep Time: **5**   Minutes

Cook Time: **5**   Minutes

Total Time: ***10***   Minutes

INGREDIENTS

- 1 bunch kale
- 1 cup cooked chickpeas
- ¼ red onion
- ¼ cup tahini
- ¼ cup lemon juice
- 1 cup salad dressing

DIRECTIONS

1. In a bowl mix all ingredients and mix well
2. Serve with dressing

Serves: 2
Prep Time: 5   Minutes

Cook Time: 5   Minutes

Total Time: 10   Minutes

INGREDIENTS

- 1 lb. tortellini
- ¼ cup olive oil
- 1 tablespoon balsamic vinegar
- 1 tsp salt
- 1 cup spinach leaves
- ½ cup Parmesan
- 1 cup tomatoes

DIRECTIONS

1. In a bowl mix all ingredients and mix well
2. Serve with dressing

TACO SALAD

Serves: **2**
Prep Time: **5**   Minutes

Cook Time: **5**   Minutes

Total Time: **10**   Minutes

INGREDIENTS

- ½ cup olive oil
- 1 lb. cooked steak
- 1 tablespoon taco seasoning
- Juice of 1 lime
- 1 tsp cumin
- 1 head romaine lettuce
- 1 cup corn
- 1 cup beans
- 1 cup tomatoes

DIRECTIONS

1. **In a bowl mix all ingredients and mix well**
2. **Serve with dressing**

DORITO TACO SALAD

Serves: 2

Prep Time: 5   Minutes

Cook Time: 5   Minutes

Total Time: **10** Minutes

INGREDIENTS

- 1 lb. cooked beef
- 1 tsp chili powder
- 1 tsp paprika
- 1 tsp cumin
- 1 head romaine lettuce
- 1 cup cherry tomatoes
- 1 cup cheddar cheese
- 1 avocado
- 1 bag doritos
- ¼ cup sour cream

DIRECTIONS

1. In a bowl mix all ingredients and mix well
2. Serve with dressing

CHEESEBURGER SALAD

Serves: **2**

Prep Time: **5**   Minutes

Cook Time: **5**   Minutes

Total Time: **10**   Minutes

INGREDIENTS

- 1 lb. cooked beef
- 1 tsp garlic powder
- 1 tsp Worcestershire sauce
- 1 tsp black pepper
- 1 cup salad dressing
- 1 head romaine lettuce
- 1 cup cheddar cheese
- 1/4 red onion
- 1 tsp sesame seeds

DIRECTIONS

1. In a bowl mix all ingredients and mix well
2. Serve with dressing

MANDARIN SALAD

Serves: 2
Prep Time: 5 Minutes
Cook Time: 5 Minutes
Total Time: 10 Minutes

INGREDIENTS

- 2 cups lettuce
- 2 cups red cabbage
- 2 cups cooked chicken
- ¼ cup carrot
- ¼ cup almonds

DRESSING

- 1 tablespoon honey
- 2 tablespoons rice wine vinegar
- 1 tablespoon soy sauce
- 1 tablespoon hoisin sauce

DIRECTIONS

1. In a bowl mix all ingredients and mix well
2. Serve with dressing

Serves: **2**

Prep Time: **5** Minutes

Cook Time: **5** Minutes

Total Time: **10** Minutes

INGREDIENTS

- 1 lb. cooked penne
- 1 can corn kernels
- 1 can beans
- 1 cup cheddar cheese
- 1 avocado
- ½ cup cilantro
- 1 cup salad dressing

DIRECTIONS

1. **In a bowl mix all ingredients and mix well**
2. **Serve with dressing**

BUTTERNUT SQUASH STEW

Serves: **4**

Prep Time: **15** Minutes

Cook Time: **45** Minutes

Total Time: **60** Minutes

INGREDIENTS

- 2 tablespoons olive oil
- 2 red onions
- 2 cloves garlic
- 1. Tablespoon rosemary
- 1 tablespoon thyme
- 2 lb. beef
- 1 cup white wine
- 1 cup butternut squash
- 2 cups beef broth
- ½ cup tomatoes

DIRECTIONS

1. Chop all ingredients in big chunks
2. In a large pot heat olive oil and add ingredients one by one
3. Cook for 5-6 or until slightly brown

4. Add remaining ingredients and cook until tender, 35-45 minutes

5. Season while stirring on low heat

6. When ready remove from heat and serve

BEEF STEW

Serves: **4**

Prep Time: **15**   Minutes

Cook Time: **45**   Minutes

Total Time: **60**   Minutes

INGREDIENTS

- 2 lb. beef
- 1 tsp salt
- 4 tablespoons olive oil
- 2 red onions
- 2 cloves garlic
- 1 cup white wine
- 2 cups beef broth
- 1 cup water
- 3-4 bay leaves
- ¼ tsp thyme
- 1 lb. potatoes

DIRECTIONS

1. Chop all ingredients in big chunks
2. In a large pot heat olive oil and add ingredients one by one
3. Cook for 5-6 or until slightly brown

4. Add remaining ingredients and cook until tender, 35-45 minutes
5. Season while stirring on low heat
6. When ready remove from heat and serve

CORN CASSEROLE

Serves: **4**

Prep Time: **10**   Minutes

Cook Time: **15**   Minutes

Total Time: **25**   Minutes

INGREDIENTS

- ½ cup cornmeal
- ½ cup butter
- 2 eggs
- 1 cup milk
- ½ cup heavy cream
- 3 cups corn
- ¼ tsp smoked paprika

DIRECTIONS

1. Sauté the veggies and set aside
2. Preheat the oven to 425 F
3. Transfer the sautéed veggies to a baking dish, add remaining ingredients to the baking dish
4. Mix well, add seasoning and place the dish in the oven
5. Bake for 12-15 minutes or until slightly brown

6. When ready remove from the oven and serve

ARTICHOKE CASSEROLE

Serves: **4**

Prep Time: **10**   Minutes

Cook Time: **15**   Minutes

Total Time: **25**   Minutes

INGREDIENTS

- 1 cup cooked rice
- 1 cup milk
- 1 cup parmesan cheese
- 4 oz. cream cheese
- 1 lb. cooked chicken breast
- 1 cup spinach
- 1 can artichoke hearts
- 1 cup mozzarella cheese

DIRECTIONS

1. Sauté the veggies and set aside
2. Preheat the oven to 425 F
3. Transfer the sautéed veggies to a baking dish, add remaining ingredients to the baking dish
4. Mix well, add seasoning and place the dish in the oven
5. Bake for 12-15 minutes or until slightly brown
6. When ready remove from the oven and serve

MUSHROOM PIZZA

Serves: **2**

Prep Time: **10**   Minutes

Cook Time: **30**   Minutes

Total Time: **40**   Minutes

INGREDIENTS

-   2 button mushrooms
-   ½ red onion
-   1 lemon juiced
-   1 tablespoon parsley
-   ½ cup ground flax seeds
-   2 tablespoons olive oil
-   1 cup almonds whole
-   1 cup cashews whole
-   1 carrot

DIRECTIONS

1. Preheat oven to 375 F and place a baking sheet
2. In food processor place all the ingredients and blend for 8-10 minutes

3. Pour the mixture on the baking sheet and bake for 15-20 minutes until golden
4. Remove from the oven and serve

CASSEROLE PIZZA

Serves: **6-8**

Prep Time: **10** Minutes

Cook Time: **15** Minutes

Total Time: **25** Minutes

INGREDIENTS

- 1 pizza crust
- ½ cup tomato sauce
- ¼ black pepper
- 1 cup zucchini slices
- 1 cup mozzarella cheese
- 1 cup olives

DIRECTIONS

1. Spread tomato sauce on the pizza crust
2. Place all the toppings on the pizza crust
3. Bake the pizza at 425 F for 12-15 minutes
4. When ready remove pizza from the oven and serve

THANK YOU FOR READING THIS BOOK!

CPSIA information can be obtained
at www.ICGtesting.com
Printed in the USA
BVHW030120270221
601199BV00001B/112